Star
Struck

David McCooey

David McCooey is an award-winning poet, critic, and editor. His debut poetry collection, *Blister Pack* (2005), won the Mary Gilmore Award and was shortlisted for four other major national literary awards. His second full-length collection, *Outside* (2011), was shortlisted for the Queensland Literary Awards and was a finalist for the Melbourne Prize for Literature's 'Best Writing Award'. His work has appeared for nine out of the last ten years in Black Inc.'s annual anthology, *The Best Australian Poems*. McCooey is the deputy general editor of the prize-winning *Macquarie PEN Anthology of Australian Literature* (2009), and he is the author of a critical study on Australian autobiography, *Artful Histories* (1996/2009), which won a NSW Premier's Literary Award. McCooey is also a musician and sound artist. His album of 'poetry soundtracks', *Outside Broadcast*, was released in 2013 as a digital download. He is a professor of writing and literature at Deakin University in Geelong, where he lives.

Poems by
David McCooey
Star
Struck

Poetry

First published in 2016 by
UWA Publishing
Crawley, Western Australia 6009
www.uwap.uwa.edu.au

UWAP is an imprint of UWA Publishing
a division of The University of Western Australia

THE UNIVERSITY OF
WESTERN
AUSTRALIA

National Library of Australia
Cataloguing-in-Publication entry:
McCooey, David Wyndham, author.
Star struck / David McCooey.
ISBN: 9781742589107 (paperback)
Australian poetry.
A821.3

Designed by Becky Chilcott, Chil3
Typeset in Lyon Text by Lasertype
Printed by McPherson's Printing Group

 uwapublishing

To the memory of my father,
Wyndham McCooey (1928–2013).

Contents

This Voice

It goes without saying
that it sounds like your voice.
But is it yours? And if
not yours, then whose?

It could be the voice-over in a film;
not a war movie, but a
tale of contingency and
darkness that begins and ends

with summer's teeming
insects starting up at night,
phantom traffic, and the
enduring noise of a goods train.

1

Documents

'Two other facts I know are these. Nobody ever confides a secret to one person only. No one destroys all copies of a document. Also, that it is children really, perhaps because so much is forbidden to them, who understand from within the nature of crime'.

Renata Adler, *Pitch Dark* (1983)

Habit

In his bedroom, your son looks at pictures
of Ancient Egypt. Dark-haired workers
moving giant blocks of stone in the pale air.
'What were the workers buried in?' he asks.
He turns the page to show jackal-headed
Anubis, presider of the weighing of the heart,
laying his hands on a pharaoh's coffin,
a brightly coloured wooden sleeping bag.
Custom is tool and pathology, you think.

And so is habit. While you set the table
at the appointed hour, laying out the cutlery,
your wife jokes with your son that you are
'a creature of habit.' After dinner, there is
the ritual of cleaning away the mess of eating.
The dog is given some half-cooked meat.
Your son has his bath, and returns wrapped
in his Egyptian-cotton towel to suggest that
you write a book called *The Monster of Habit*.

In the morning, dressed in his gaudy pyjamas,
he builds with his mother a room-sized construction
out of chairs, cushions, and blankets,
filled with unblinking stuffed toys and plastic jewels.
They are playing tomb raiders. You are invited in.
In your sacerdotal dressing gown, you get on
your hands and knees to enter the labyrinth.
You are shown the bewitching everyday things
that have been set aside for the afterlife.

Speaking the Language

And then one day you appear
in Accident and Emergency.

You state your concerns,
and you're rushed through,

like you're holding a special pass.
You are put on a bed and hooked

to a machine that soon confirms
a cardiac event. Almost as if

they were not yours, tears start
coursing down the side of your face.

'What's the matter?' a doctor asks.
'I'm just labile,' you say,

and the doctor is satisfied.
You are speaking his language.

Music for Hospitals

i)
Sunday morning.
The sound of church bells;
a patient answers her phone.

ii)
Nurses recalibrating equipment:
'Four, five, six become
seven, eight, nine.'

iii)
The elderly patient leaves
his TV on all afternoon
while reading the paper.

iv)
When told his patient's
former weight, the bearded
nurse yells 'That's massive!'

v)
Everything happens at once:
a nurse with a needle;
the synaesthesia of breakfast.

vi)
The doctor appears with his
silent, staring students: graduates
from *The Village of the Damned*.

Cardiac Ward Poetics

1. Hospital light, like any other
light, is rarely 'lemon-coloured'.

2. Any verse form will do, but
the catalogue may seem most apt.

3. Try to remember
everybody's name.

4. Loretta, Alison, Ron,
someone, someone.

5. Anecdote lends
itself to a satirical tone.

6. Satire is the audacious
mode of the healthy.

7. Words to avoid: 'bravura',
'filigree', 'burnished'. The usual.

8. Is there any need to be so
Spartan about everything?

9. Nausea, more than pain,
is poetry's teeming limit.

The Hunter

When you were young,
the nurse would have been
called a 'male nurse'.
The patient opposite—
middle-aged and jockey-thin—
cracks small jokes
through his shifts.

The nurse is short, thirty-something,
and excellent at taking blood.
His arms are pale and hairless.
On the last day, as you are packing,
he approaches like a conspirator.

With a phone in his outstretched hand
he flicks through a small cache of images.
There he is dressed in fatigues
with *Apocalypse Now* face paint;
there his guns rest on a bed of grass;
there he stands with a fellow hunter;
and there lies a pretty, long-legged animal
on the bonnet of a four-wheel drive.
You sense him searching
your face as you look.

Then he turns to the other patient,
who is sitting in bed in his striped pyjamas
and too far away to see anything.
He holds the phone aloft like an offering
or a promise.

Invisible Cities

i)
Back home from hospital again.
You read *Invisible Cities* outside
in the morning sun. A small lizard appears.
Its solar-powered musculature moves
across the paving stones. Its skin is both matte
and jewelled in the sunlight. It stops and flicks
its front legs down to its sides, like an ingenious
Edwardian gadget snapping itself shut.
You and the creature take in the sun, then
the lizard heads for the maze of grass,
hiding from the hard-nosed suburban birds.
You take yourself indoors into the dark of the house,
clutching Calvino, the old fabulist.

ii)
Later, the sun performs its drawn-out
power-down, summer already merciless.
You take the dog for a walk, its gait ginger,
while it fusses over what to piss on.
Around the corner, the audacious stadium lights
vie against the sunset. The smell of frying meat
is in the air; the bitter taste of Anginine
under your tongue.

iii)
You read at night, while a lawless wind
upsets the house. You lose your thread.
Calvino engenders fantasies. Dark staircases
frequented by music students and government men;
a forest in which night squats;
an empty Ferris wheel, with all its moral weight.

The dog in his fur
sleeps on dusty floorboards,
and twitches like a muscle.

Animal Studies

You read a story about a mouse,
which—in addition to the mouse—
features a woman, a man, and a cat.

The cat reminds you of the moment
in one of the Canterbury Tales,
in which a man, a monk perhaps,

pushes a cat off a seat, so he may sit on
the warmth left by the cat's body
(which is the same as saying 'the cat').

You remember in turn your first year
at university: your Middle English tutor
drew the class's attention

to this moment, a recognisably
human action, something familiar
from that alien medievalism.

This memory—these memories—come
to you almost three decades later,
your own personal Middle Ages.

You remember, too, how that same tutor
invited the class to his home
for an end-of-year barbecue:

meat frying in the suburban Spring air;
two pale stone cats by the fly-screen door.
You left early, despite your tutor's

evident hospitality—he had
shown you photos of the renovation
of his 1950's house. It was to see

your girlfriend, you had feebly said.
And now your ex-tutor
has emailed out of the blue

to ask if you could assess
a PhD thesis, in animal studies,
which you decline for 'health reasons'.

You remind him of the barbecue,
and he in turn recalls your leaving early.
Apologies all round, and Time

again shows its strangely patient nature.
The tale about the mouse ends with
the woman throwing the half-dead mouse,

caught in the trap she had laid, into
the unmoved snow outside her house.
And this reminds you of a time

involving a real mouse that you had caught
inside a cardboard box
(though there is no memory

explaining how that came about).
Like the woman in the story,
you were afraid of killing that creature

of fur and soft bones, finally
deciding upon the miserable
coup de grâce of smothering it in sand

from your child's clam-shaped sandpit,
knowing then your ancient,
human cowardice—

as if a choking mouse would have cared.
That memory, the cat, waited so long outside the
un-renovated mouse-hole of your life.

Callings

You wake up
to an email from your sister.
Your father is gravely ill.
And so, now, is the morning.

...

You call your sister,
and it begins, the sick little poem
that you will never write,
its endless petitions.

...

You phone your father
that last time. His voice
is unrecognisable,
a thespian's geriatric.

...

At the funeral,
after the Goldberg Aria,
your golden-haired son
cries out for food.

...

In these years since, you resist,
almost successfully,
the desire to fill
the orphaned silence.

Not to Disturb

To knock at the door,
one must first make a fist.

But it is not Death in
his outdated apparel at your

doorstep, only your boss, doing
the right thing. You make

tea and offer him pale biscuits,
which you no longer eat.

But your heart isn't in
this executive socialising.

Your real heart—a fist-sized
muscle, supposedly—knocks

at the walls of your chest
as you see off your visitor,

and return to your reading:
Muriel Spark's *Not to Disturb*.

A little dated, but death-filled
in its comedy of manners.

One Way or Another

They can't give you a date
for your bypass operation.
Before Christmas,
if you are lucky.

'We'll be in touch
each Wednesday
to let you know
one way or another.'

And so your future
waits, somewhere
outside, while you
sit inside and re-read

Muriel Spark: *The Takeover,*
Territorial Rights,
The Driver's Seat.
You read them obsessively

each night, as insects
swarm under street lights,
free of consciousness
and futurity.

You see in the New Year,
and time passes,
your nervous system
a shivering horse within you.

But everything can wait,
one way or another,
as you discovered in earlier
visits to the cardiology ward.

The 'code blue' announcements
and even the arrival of
ambulances at A and E
downstairs were less rushed,

more stately, than you
would ever have expected.
Just like the helicopter
outside your ward

those times—lifting off
into the night air,
heavy, and unhurried,
towards some unseen future.

The Questionnaire

Earlier that year
you had been sent
a questionnaire
about poetry and illness.

'Which poets would
you turn to if you
were unwell?' That
sort of thing.

In your five admissions
to hospital, the only
poetry you read was
Tomas Tranströmer's

Selected Poems.
Like everything, it is
hard to say why. Perhaps
because of the poems'

attention to darkness,
their foreign land.
Because of the seasons;
the dark lakes; the houses

caught within cars' headlights;
reality, like a great ship,
brightly lit
on the night's horizon.

And there was the book's cover,
its cream pages;
the author's alliterative name,
with its one diacritic

(twin moons above their
empty planet).
One time, you noted
that the missing 'H'

of 'TOMAS'
was painted in the circle
on the ground
outside your ward,

where the helicopter landed,
mostly at night,
in the great hollow
of its visceral noise.

The Point

Heartless Christmas over,
you and your wife head to Mornington,
where cafes are open,
and strangers sit at tables
or walk down the street
in their dark or bright clothes,
occult as ever.

You see a movie,
a weepie about a couple on a quest.
Afterwards, in the car-park
behind the cinema, you and
your wife share tearing words,
the mysterious etiology of anger.

You sit in the car, listening
to the sound of a woman crying,
watching clouds in the cinematic sky,
the cars patient in the sun,
like beasts waiting for their owners.

There is a finger pressed
against your breastbone,
and left there, long after
the point has been made.

Intensive Care (i)

You come to life in the half-light,
a swaddled infant. You watch the nurses—
one to a patient—watching their

glowing devices throughout the night.
An old woman wails interminably;
you growl softly inside yourself.

When you wake again your adult daughter,
impassive with her smart phone, sits
by your bedside in the phenomenal morning.

You inhabit the country of nausea,
from where you fervidly refuse medication.
You take your first post-operative walk,

a century of steps through the ICU,
with human and mechanical aid.
Someone tells you that the old woman

has been moved to her ward.
But there was a death in the night,
one of the younger nurses quite upset about it.

Intensive Care (ii)

There had been an earlier
waking,
in the ICU,

a time you have
deeply forgotten,
when you had the worst

of it—the pain, the detubation,
the harrowing scenes
of your return to life.

Your wife witnessed it,
graphically laying it out to
you some weeks later,

so that you were both
gifted with that
pointless knowledge.

Second-Person

Delivered by green-clad
medical staff to this place,

you enter the realm
of the second-person singular,

a new you
to ghost the old,

the one on the other side
of a recalibrated life:

a body lying in
a bed, alive to

the homespun sounds of
each unprecedented sunrise.

2

Available Light

'Thus if we see the pictures clearly as photographs, we will perhaps also see, or sense, something of their other, more private, willful, and anarchic meanings'.

John Szarkowski, *William Eggleston's Guide* (1976)

Early Photographs

View from the window at Le Gras.
Self-portrait as a drowned man.
Boulevard du Temple, Paris 1838.
Louis Dodier as a prisoner.
Untitled (two women posed with a chair).
Use of ether for anaesthesia.
Valley of the shadow of death.
Untitled (melancholia passing into mania).
The ladder. Reclining nude.
The ascent of Mont Blanc via a crevice.
The Prince Imperial on a pony beneath a window.
Communards in their coffins.
Miss Booth; Miss Booth.
The Moon: Considered as a Planet, a World, and a Satellite.
Synoptic table of the forms of the nose.
The open door. The horse in motion.

Available Light

Office blocks thrust
into buffeting daylight;

houses hunker under
pale suburban skies;

a low-slung cat crosses
the photographic dusk;

the science-fiction lighting
of deserted 7-Elevens;

the out-dated starlight;

a nightwalker passes
the TV-blue of windows;

a phosphorescent Frisbee
muses on the porch;

sentinel LEDs on consoles
and microwave clock;

fridge glow upon the subtle
slate and stainless steel;

the mirrors' unnatural magic.

Scene From a Marriage

A man and a woman
walking on a beach.

Their small child runs
across the hard, wet sand
of the intertidal zone,
from one parent to the other.

A strange dog barks
at the waves, or the wind,
or at nothing.

Now the child—unrelenting—
is wanting to be carried.

The car park in the distance;
a scattering of vehicles
in a cold, unsentimental light.

Summer Nights, Walking

Orderly lawns; licorice power lines;
the becalmed trees.
Your neighbour's patio displays
two white plastic chairs.
Statuesque cars curated
by the street lights.
You walk, as if blameless,
through the indulgent dark.

A bat leathers past,
like it's learning to fly.
At Barwon Boulevard the steep slope
to the river gradates to darkness.
Muted noises betray
night's unkempt life below.

Poem

The seasonal Ferris wheel, down by
  the waterfront, operates late
    into the summer evenings.

Two or three groups are taken
  each time into the cooler air above,
    into that dark space where one can

properly appreciate the bitter
  industrial lights across the bay,
    or the unlit hearts of Moreton Bays below.

At the wheel's apex we see
  the figures of a couple, loitering by
    the kitschy bollards and palm trees

on the far-below of the footpath—
  impossibly solid—like they
    didn't have a care in the underworld.

Three Hysterical Short Stories

1.
The boys had been down to the river.
Something had happened there,
but they won't say what.

'Tell me! Tell me!' yells the father
to the eldest child, who remains silent
in the failing light of the early evening.

2.
It is the hottest day of the year.
The trees in the suburban street
cast their ineffectual shadows.

A large white car appears across the road
from our house. A middle-aged couple
sit in the car, the windows wound down.

'How can they stand this heat?'
my mother says. I imagine there's
a revolver in the car's glove-box.

The car sits beneath the shade of the
peppermint gum, it seems, for hours.
My mother peers out the lounge window.

The car remains. The couple drink
from a large plastic bottle, smoke cigarettes,
occasionally get out to stretch their legs.

'If they don't leave soon I'm calling
your father,' my mother says, as I sit on the floor
in front of the fan, watching day-time TV.

Some time later, my father is running late.
'What are they doing there?' my mother shouts,
loud enough to be heard across the road, I think.

The late afternoon is orange-coloured.
There is a fire in the hills. Finally, the car starts.
It has just driven out of sight when my father returns.

3.
Miles and Veronica sit beneath
the concrete water tower.
Trees across the road sway in the breeze.

Veronica has packed food. Despite the heat,
they sit on an old picnic rug
that she has brought from her father's house.

Miles says things, and Veronica says things.
The whole time Miles picks
and picks at the dry grass beside the rug.

After a pause, Miles and Veronica say more things.
Birds come and go, as they do.
Finally, Miles walks to the car. He is shouting.

He throws his phone to the ground, hard.
Veronica shouts something at him.
The water tower maintains its silence.

The Dolls' House

(i) Mise en scène

It is a bourgeois house: three storeys;
  pitched roof; casement windows, free of glass.
Like a house in a European war, the entire
  back wall has been sheared off.

(But the yellow roof is sound.) Upstairs there is
  a balcony to suggest distance. On the ground floor
is the kitchen (a pie nearly cooked),
  a table, three chairs, and an over-sized high chair.

A clock keeps watch above an empty desk.
  It is just past one-fifteen. The phone has
not worked for years. In the generous
  bathroom, there is a mirror smeared with dim.

Like a cruel joke, the house has no stairs.
  In the bedroom on the top storey, there is
a bed, pink with girlhood, and a baby's cot
  that will not rock. (The parents have no bed.)

The family is a traditional family. They can
  move their arms and bend at the waist,
so that they may bow, or sit down
  to eat their meals of dust and sunlight.

(ii) Father

Casually dressed, he is the tallest of the household.
He wears a wristwatch, though its face is opaque,
    since he cannot turn his wrist.
Unlike his blonde family,
        he has serious brown hair,
        lacquered like the early 1960s.

He sits in front of the television,
    with his fixed smile.
If you look closely,
    you will see he does not view the screen.
Instead, he is gazing off into the middle distance.
His eyes are night-black, with pinpoints of white.
He and his wife, the same in this respect,
        have given their eyes
        to their children.

(iii) Mother

She has a bust and hips, so that
    her children can recognise her.
Her silver earrings are 'for herself'.
Unlike her husband, but not her children,
    her lips are pink.
Her legs are bare from below the knee.

Like the astronomer Tycho Brahe,
    she has lost her nose.
She watches the night sky
    as best she can from the kitchen table.
Like Brahe and his assistant Kepler,
        she has no telescope,
            relying only on her naked eye.
She doesn't tell her husband, but she is
    close to deducing the laws of planetary motion.

(iv) Daughter

A smaller version of her mother,
   her unruly hair signifies youth.
She is being home-schooled, and she
      is never bored. No-one
      has taught her how to be lonely.
She has so much to learn.

In her free time she likes to stand
   at the balcony, romantically.
She imagines what she would see
      if she were to fall from there,
      onto the endless plain below.
Perhaps, she thinks, she could
   take herself away to be raised by wolves,
   and follow tracks in powder-soft snow.
She would like to learn how to sleep.

(v) Baby

Let us suppose that he is a boy,
   all children being in need of a pronoun.
He is the family comedian, with his
      lick of blonde hair
      on an otherwise-bald head.
He can stand, but not yet walk.

He watches his family every moment.
He is the apple of his father's eye,
   never crying or calling out at night.
Like his sister, he only pretends to sleep,
      wiling away the hours
      by eyeing off the plastic toys
      next to his sister's bed.
He hears his mother downstairs in the kitchen,
   gently coughing in the astigmatic night.

Grand Designs

With his mocking Tudor ways—
creepy ginger beard and historical girth—

the wife knows that if there were cameras
rolling now they would be embarrassed

by his grand designs. She looks at her kitchen,
her garden. How odd that the indefinite article

cosies up to 'domestic' so sinisterly. She remembers
being young to all this, when love thatched her.

Rhyming 1970s

He sits on his bed, listening to a cassette,
while watching on the silent tv set
a black-and-white silent Jacqueline Bisset,
and dimly hearing, from the kitchenette
his mother list the things with which she's beset.

Georges Perec: A True Story

A, who has been chronically unwell,
is going to her appointment.

B, her husband, is walking
C, their child, to school,
taking D, their dog, with them.

(E is away; out of town.)

B, C, and D walk through
the summer morning air.

C talks his innocent talk.

B keeps his thoughts to himself.

When they approach the school,
C puts his face up to be kissed,
and then runs off to the school gate.

Walking away with D,
B's mobile phone rings.

He feels a stab of alarm.

He fumbles with the device,
and answers the call.

It is A.

'Yes? What is it?' B says,
unable to sound entirely calm.

A has a question.

'What is the name of that
French author who writes
proceduralist novels?'

The Cat's Pyjamas

are laid out on the bed.
They are old, but clean,
and neatly folded.
They have the rumour
of wardrobe about them.
Their napped cotton
is like the pelt
of a small animal.
But the cat is nowhere
to be seen. He has
taken off, once again,
into the brittle night,
smart phone pressed
to the triangle of his ear.

Europe

The grey and the green
under the white of the sky,
and over the black of the earth.

The annual pogrom of Autumn.

Soldiers in the fog;
soldiers marching
in the guiltless dusk.

The storybook animals
living in bungalows.

Night birds singing
their repetitive songs.

Election

'We move like gazelles or the way gazelles move in a tiger's dream'
Roberto Bolaño, *By Night in Chile* (trans Chris Andrews)

Who were we? some wondered
on that election night, as we
watched or did not watch the
television, listened or did not
listen to the victory speech
made for us in the mild Spring
night, not so unlike other nights.

Who were we? some wondered
as we saw, or did not see,
the news about the boats
for which we afforded ourselves
so little responsibility, our
island coasts so dear, so costly,
'for those who've come across the seas'.

Who were we? we wondered,
or did not wonder, as we saw,
or did not see, the news about
the OPCs at Manus Island and Nauru,
Reza Berati's death, those in despair,
the children going insane. Who
were *we* to think these not ours?

'Whaling Station' Redux

i)
What trash, that poem of mine about the whaling station
we visited in Albany in the primitive 1970s, those years
when an operational slaughterhouse could be a family
tourist attraction. My late father's legacy of 35mm slides,
newly digitised, undoes my poem, with three shots—
miraculous and amoral—of butchered whales,
a shock defacement of poetry's mouthy reckoning.

ii)
In the first capture, there are winches, wire, a stone wheel
(for sharpening things, I imagine), rust-coloured concrete,
a fibro building, and the figures of two blue-singleted men
in gumboots, one bending, both partly obscured by steam rising
from blocks of whale meat. The steam has a pink colouration.

iii)
The second capture suffers from camera shake,
that analogue of nausea, and shows two men with metal bars
prying into the whale's remains. Above them are
the innocent clouds, a seabird with extended wings.

iv)
In the third capture, two boys are in the frame. They could be,
but are not, my brother and me. They are looking at a single carcass:
headless, flayed, and eviscerated, the mess of it
rendered into dreadful blacks, reds, and whites.
In the centre of the whale the JPEG clips to pure black.

v)
I was five years old when I was taken to witness this industry of men.
When I show my father's photographs to my six-year-old son,
I skip past these three images, momentarily panicky.
My blonde son, intent on the screen, wants to know what
he's just seen, but does not argue when I tell him it's not for him.
We move on to a grainy shot of Uncle Mac—who was no blood relation,
but shared my father's name—standing before the Arc de Triomphe.

Sandwich Meat

What will cure me
  of this taste for
thinly sliced animals—
  pink and white and grey—
on the soft lunar surface
  of sourdough bread?

Letter to Ken Bolton

Dear Ken, tonight there was a power blackout
at our place, during which Maria and I watched
Fiona Shaw perform *The Waste Land* in an app
on our iPad (which was luckily fully charged).
Her performance was electrifying (har har),
changing voices like a dial sweeping across a radio.

Unlike Eliot's adenoidal readings of the poem, Shaw
treated the poem as theatre. I'd never thought about
how Madame Sosostris would sound *with a cold*.
So there Maria and I were, with our electronic device
and three candles in a darkened house, like some
eighteenth-century tableau, a fact we both noted

more or less simultaneously, commenting on
the disjunction between the technologies.
'The domestic postmodern' one of us called it
(the quote marks inevitably hanging in the air).
Meanwhile, Shaw's presentation of Eliot's poem
brought out new shades previously unnoticed:

how 'Falling towers' reads post-9/11; how those
'hooded hordes' evoke Hollywood Islamophobia; and
how camp ('queer' even) the poem could be
(and not just because of the bit about Mr Eugenides).
Shaw made *The Waste Land* strangely sexy; the
Cockneys in 'A Game of Chess' funny and tragic.

Actually, the blackout was a brownout, according
to the man from the power company who I called
on our out-dated Nokia mobile phone. (Students go
into raptures of nostalgia when I look at the phone
in class.) But 'brownout' doesn't sound quite
so lyrical, does it? It has an embarrassingly

scatological sound to it (or let's just say 'shittiness',
which is more James Joyce than T.S. Eliot). Or else
it evokes the War, meaning the Second World War,
my parents' war, my father turning eighteen
years of age in nineteen forty-six. But in the forties
I don't suppose they had clothes dryers to turn off

during a brownout so as not to burn out the motors.
And our brownout didn't last long, just enough
to make the night seem strange—reading to my son
by torchlight, boiling water for tea on the stove-top,
peering through the blinds at our darkened street,
the street lights looking uncertain. But by eight-thirty

'service had returned to normal'. I was answering work
emails, and thinking about writing this letter
(this 'verse epistle') to you, who I don't know well
but whose voices (those that occupy your books)
have kept me amused and aglow, like a boy with
his ear against a radio in the war, valves warm

in the night, the room filled with interesting
and recondite thoughts. *P.S.* By coincidence,
I have a copy of Bolaño's *The Savage Detectives*
on my bedside table, a novel which features in
one of your verse letters. All of your writing shows
that such coincidences are the stuff of art (where are

those quote marks?), every thought and every action
jostling together like bumper cars or comedians or
paratroopers drifting down from the sky like beautiful
mushrooms, and being fired upon by grim-faced Nazis below,
their automatic weapons ripping through the delicate night,
all a diversion for the Resistance to blow up the power station.

Night Squibs

i) Sam's Nightmare

Our six-year-old son
has had a nightmare.
He had lost us,
and couldn't find us,
despite his frantic searching.

'Where did this happen?' we ask.
'At a literary festival,' he says.

ii) Middle Age

Lying in bed,
listening to the fireworks.

iii) Human Nature

By the light of the bedside lamp
I flick through
Last Words of the Executed.

iv) The War on Terror

The night rumbles outside.
On the late news:
'Police stormed the granny flat.'

v) Noël

The night before Christmas
I insert batteries into
my son's automatic rifle.

Darkness Speaks

None of it is true: I am
neither malevolent nor

mystical. You have nothing
to fear; I am the one who makes

things bright and
dramatic when they need to be.

Like when I spill myself a
little at sunset. Night after

night you dream of me. One day
you will wake up for good,

and there I will be, at last.
Your new and endless climate.

Don't look at me; I don't compose
any *kindertotenlieder.*

3

Pastorals (Eighteen Dramatic Monologues)

'Probably the cases I take are the surprising rather than the normal ones, and once started on an example I follow it without regard to the unity of the book.'

William Empson, *Some Versions of Pastoral* (1935)

Apple Corps Ltd

for Susan Baker

When I worked for the Beatles,
the office wasn't as chaotic as
some made out later; the 60s
mostly happened on television.
Meanwhile, in Savile Row, Paul was
brilliant and humble, shepherding everyone
through the days, though you could tell he
had a streak of passive aggression,
or at least we would have thought that if
we'd had that phrase up our sleeves.
John was charming and bitter,
a slave to his moods. George was
surprisingly like John in that regard,
but hid it better. Ringo, as all the
books say, just wanted everyone
to get on. The fans weren't a problem.
They were young and shy, extras in an
unlikely pastoral, paperbacks clutched
to their chests. We were all fans, of course,
and we loved the music like we were
married to it. Now the songs are packing their
bags for the museum, and we are
proud and a little sad, like the first time
we heard 'Mother Nature's Son'.

Mick and Bianca Jagger, Newlyweds

We are in the back of the Bentley;
the church and the Riviera crowds
are behind us. The sunroof is open.
The whirring photographer, bundled
in the car with us, clutching his Leica,
is getting this performance, this evanescent
mood, for posterity. Priapic champagne
bottle and all. Then we speed past
a field, the greenest I've ever seen.
The marriage is already over. But I will
only think about the first time we kissed,
in the grey stairwell on that winter's
day. We had stood for a minute, maybe two.
The only thing touching were our lips.

How To Be a Better Elvis

The Parkes Observatory, surrounded by
its wheat and alien sheep, listens to the stars.
The town statue of the Founding Father looks
to be singing or preaching, an over-sized book in hand.
In January, the Elvis Festival herds in
the over-weight men, the Priscilla look-alikes,
the memorabilia's promise of a Golden Age.

I'm not interested in the Vegas era.
I return each summer like an old-time itinerant,
getting younger every year, reaching back,
until I find that boy in a Tupelo shotgun shack,
crazy for music and listening for God.

Nightbird Singing

I guess you could say I am
something of a Stevie Nicks fan.
This is the second time I have
seen her in concert. The first
time I went with a couple of
girlfriends. Tonight my husband
has come along. Years ago,
he and I would listen to *Bella Donna*
half the night away, at least
on those weekends his cronies
weren't around. The last concert we
saw together was Neil Young.
I like his country songs, but his voice
is too whiney, and his electric stuff
too loud and a bit nasty. Anyhow,
what I like about Stevie is how,
whether she's out there dressed
as a witch or a shepherdess, she's
always kind of real. You can learn
a lot about men and women from
her songs—the complaints and
the ecstasies. I reckon her time at
Arcadia High School wasn't that
different from my school days,
even if I was in Colorado and not
California. My friends and I used to
wear the same platform boots as Stevie
when we went out on the weekend.
My husband would like me to get
those out one night, I shouldn't wonder.
You know, when Stevie checked herself
into the Betty Ford Center, I couldn't
have been happier for her.

Before and After Science
(Brian Eno in Hospital)

The sound of a dog barking
is the sound of the space the dog is in.
Or so I think for the moment,
alone in my private room,
hearing those dull metal sounds that sound
in the gap between visiting hours.

I slowly rise, make my way across
the room to the record player,
and gently place the needle onto
the record that Judy brought in.

Back on my bed of olive-green
I realise the music is too quiet.
Too much gain reduction, as the engineers
say in their paradoxical style.
Only the right channel is audible, so that
the harp music sounds like water.

I do not move. I see power lines;
the faint green of a distant park;
clouds moving, just perceptibly.
Rain may or may not be in the air.

Monody: Joni Mitchell Recalls Laurel Canyon

for Michael Myshack

I arrived just after the Manson murders, in another part of the hills, when everyone locked the doors of their cul-de-sac homes.

Some nights I would think of the day in Canada when I gave away my child.

I left for Malibu before those other killings in Wonderland Avenue.

Had I come to the Hills because of the names, the poetry of it all?

Mostly now I remember the endless talking; the songs we wrote so quickly, in answer to one another.

Why should I not prize words, despite the times, like some love-sick swain?

Where but in language would you find *cloudberries, ukulele, riverbed,* and *dépaysement*?

How else would I save the canyon now, as I recall it best: the lens-flare of afternoon driving, as the sun stretch'd out all the hills?

Elegy: Tori Amos Growing Up in Maryland

When I was a child,
the noises that came out
of the television every night
made their way down the hallway
to my darkened bedroom:
hysterical laughter; shouts
of anger; gun fire and
car crashes; fighting children.
And every night the weeping,
the lamentable weeping.

Pink Moon

I was staying in a Tuscan bed-and-breakfast.
On my second day, a young Italian couple
approached me, shyly asking if I was
Nick Drake's sister. (I never know how
people find this out.) 'Yes,' I answered,
'I'm Gabrielle Drake,' not adding that I was
once the more famous. In my silver catsuit
and purple wig I was Lieutenant Ellis,
Moonbase commander on *UFO*. Three
decades later and Nick was the one having
a documentary made about him. It was
sad and beautiful, just like Nick, who'd
thought himself such a failure, especially
after *Pink Moon* made its appearance.
As if making the apocalypse sound like
a shepherd's lullaby wasn't enough...
The Italian couple were endearingly solemn,
but as always, at such moments, I didn't
know what was required of me. I looked
across the expensive pool towards the green
of the hills and said, 'I think Nick would have
loved this.' They looked at me like I was an alien.

Never For Ever

I am walking through the Woolley Building at Sydney University,
about to see my supervisor, Pippa, to talk about my doctoral thesis,
'Nature and Revolution in Blake's *Visions of the Daughters of Albion*'.
I've been struggling with Blake's ambiguous heroine, Oothoon,
sufferer of sexual violence, proponent of free love, and prophetic voice
raised against all forms of enslavement and hypocrisy.

I remember at our previous meeting, Pippa made tea for the two of us
in her office. The marked-up draft of my chapter sat on her desk.
'What's your favourite Kate Bush album?' she asked out of the blue.
We'd never spoken about music before. '*Hounds of Love*,' I said,
adding that I have a soft spot for *Never For Ever*, wondering
if this would diminish my musical acuity in my supervisor's eyes.

'I love its songs of passion and vengeful women,' I blurted, feeling naff.
'And I love how the album's cover art blends the rustic and the gothic.'
A world of monsters, butterflies, and birdlife streams from under Kate's skirt.
Pippa smiled enigmatically, and then asked if I thought the video clip
for 'Babooshka' was 'problematic' in its self-sexualisation.
Before I could answer, she started to talk about the head of discipline.

Now, as I make my way through the rabbit-warren that is the Woolley,
I struggle to think of an answer, thinking instead of Pippa's high heels.
And as I reach the end of the corridor where Pippa's office is,
I see that she has pinned (for me?) a picture of a young Kate Bush
surrounded by ivy, and in my mind bursts Oothoon's awakening:
'The moment of desire! The moment of desire!'

The Ballad of Easy Rider

It was the winter of 1982, but the 60s
were our Arcadia. We had long hair,
and we were sitting inside a barely furnished flat,
south of the river: Jeremy, Mark, Carl, and me.

Our host, Rod, had a copy of *Easy Rider* on VHS.
We got stoned pretty much straight away.
The movie wasn't what I expected. The opening
was okay: flyovers, red dirt, and lens flares.

Then Jack Nicholson's character got beaten to death
and that was a downer. I was wishing I was at home
when the front door opened, letting in cold air
and the sound of someone carrying plastic bags.

A middle-aged woman appeared, took us in,
and headed to the kitchen next to the lounge.
There was the sound of things being slammed
on a bench, and then the woman reappeared.

'Are you on drugs?' she said. Rod was like
a sand statue, indifferent to the winds of time.
'It's his mother,' whispered Jeremy, too loudly,
and as if none of us could have guessed.

'If you're not on drugs then get up,' she added.
We avoided her gaze. *Easy Rider* was still going,
its two protagonists lying dead on the highway,
black smoke rising from their burning motorcycles.

Jeremy rose from his beanbag, as if a spell had broken.
'We'll be off then,' he said, like we were leaving
afternoon tea. He gave me and Carl encouraging kicks
and got us all outside into the bright and ragged air.

We piled into Jeremy's orange Torana. As we drove off
Carl asked if we'd seen Toni Basil's name in the credits.
'What a transformation,' said Mark, and we all pissed
ourselves, bursting into the intro to 'Mickey'

like ecstatic and out-of-tune cheerleaders.
The freeway beneath us raced the dark river
all the way to the wintry city, which shone
like the future on a tilting horizon.

Genesis

It was 1983. I was going out with Marcel. He used
to deal, and it was no great surprise when he dropped out
of Arts. I followed soon after, but I didn't care.
Most warm days we'd sit in his parents' overgrown
garden and smoke until our lips burnt. And then we would
go inside, light incense, and make love. I was hoping
to get a place of our own, but Marcel was happy
living with his parents. Marcel's friends mostly hung
around because of the drugs. There was Mark, Carl,
Jeremy, Roland, and Dave, who was still in high school.
Occasionally we would take acid, the guys gazing
at the ends of their lit cigarettes. One time, Dave mildly
freaked out over how the grass outside in the night light
looked like 'blood and guts'. After calming him down,
Marcel stood on his bed and began to proclaim.

'In the beginning God created drums; everyone knows that.
These drums called down from the trees the first man.
This man played the drums until his hands were raw.
But one day, picking over the guts and bones of a
dead wildebeest, he invented the guitar. At this,
the Lord God appeared. "Who are you?" asked the man,
and the Lord God spake: "I am your manager."
The first man played his guitar, and the Lord heard
that it was good. But the street-smart man said,
"It would sound better with the drums." So the Lord God
filled the grass with the rasping sound of cicadas.
"What's that?" asked the man. "A drum machine,"
answered God. The man played to this incessant sound,
but felt there was still something lacking, so the Lord God
invented the first woman, and the first man looked
at her and said, "You can play bass."

And the man and the woman and the cicadas played
day and night, and the beasts of the earth, large and small,
would gather to listen, until one day the man appeared
by himself, without his instrument, and addressed the beasts:
"The woman and I will no longer play together."
And hearing this, the Lord God appeared, and said
"Why is this so?" And the man answered,
"Because of musical differences." And God became angry,
casting the man and the woman into the world,
telling them they would now have to work and have children,
which would make playing music impossible.'

'Then what happened?' asked Carl. 'I don't fucking know,'
said Marcel, no longer interested in his performance.
There was a moment of silence and then Jeremy
started raving about drummers. They all started dropping
names. I rarely joined in, but this time I said that Phil Collins
was a good drummer. They heaped shit on me, until I
got up and put on *The Lamb Lies Down on Broadway*.
And they shut the fuck up.

Jim Morrison's Aubade

You grab my morning
hard-on, and we are borne

to the immortal motel
where we will lodge

a brief lifetime, sheltering
from an Egyptian sun,

burning down upon
the gravestones

in the withered cemetery.
The feathered Indian

chants ecstatic outside
our door, until the end

of the banal frenzy, which
returns us to this bungalow,

an azure morning,
the day's first beer.

Alt-Country

for Cameron Lowe

I sit with Kim and Mark on the broken couch.
Blank pioneers, we drink beer and watch television
with the sound turned down, while
Tomorrow the Green Grass plays on the stereo.

After a bit, Mark and I go across the highway
to the over-lit servo, where we buy cigarettes.
A petrol tanker throbs in the night. We head back
to the house, blowing smoke into the cold air.

Kim is waiting for us on the wooden patio when we return.
'Did you get milk?' she says to Mark. 'You're fucking hopeless,'
she says. Then she takes the cigarette out of my mouth,
puts it in hers, and smiling at me, inhales deeply.

Later, when I get home, I sit in my car awhile,
listening to the hilarity and gunfire coming from
my next-door neighbour's TV, thinking my cowboy
thoughts by the thin blue light of the dashboard.

Bob Dylan's Ninth Eclogue

for Andrew Ford

Time is a grafter, stealing it all,
even your heavenly memory.

When I was young I would sing
all the live-long summer days

songs I cannot now recall,
and now my voice is shot.

And oh now my voice
has gone to the dogs.

But you can hear those
old songs any time you like,

migrated to a thousand
Spotify playlists.

Vienna

It is a Sunday in 1982. I am watching *Countdown*.
My parents are in the kitchen working on
the roast beef and Yorkshire pudding as
Molly Meldrum interviews Ultravox.

With their ties and pressed white clothes,
they look and sound like
something delicious from
an Evelyn Waugh TV adaptation.

'We're a very apolitical band,'
says Midge Ure in his 1930's getup.
I take in the 1980s and its facile
Fascist stylings. New Order, Spandau Ballet.

'This means nothing to me.' As if.
I lap it up. Yesterday, in my unlined
great coat and secondhand trilby hat,
I'd stalked through the heat of Hay St Mall.

Nature Boy

There was a boy band
on the big screen,
moving in synchronised sincerity.
I sat at the bar,
wearing my new dress,
and wondered why we
always argue on holidays.
The umbrella relaxed
in my drink, and
the pool outside
glowed unnaturally blue.
The gin was doing its work
when the man next to me
started talking, as if he
had something
important to say.
I imagined you appearing
by my side, unshaven
and bare-footed,
with that old look on your face,
shyly whispering in my ear.
Love of my life,
let's see if we have found
a path through the jungle
of our memories.
You old fool, I thought.
When will you ever learn?

Down Under

I was in an ill-lit bar in Seville
reading a newspaper report.
The Australian treasurer was
upholding his department's use
of violence. 'My cockatoo brain
screeches in my eucalypt body,'
I slurred, as I tipped the black-haired
Andalusian bartender.

I was wintering in Tahiti.
I got an email from the Australian
Ministry for the Arts announcing
their new security unit, which was
running a competition to choose
a motto. 'Our dingo liberty,'
I murmured, gazing at the
black sand of Lafayette Beach.

In a hotel lobby in Swansea
a flat-screen TV told me that
the Australian Immigration
Minister would not be moved.
A live-cross showed him
professing: 'My heart
is as dark as a newly opened
jar of Vegemite.'

Shock the Monkey

I watch the tailless ones. They have machines
for noise; not, I think, for scientific purposes.

They grimace, make mournful and
growling noises, and sometimes hit things.

I handle my food, my tail. The big
primates move slowly in pale coats.

My metal cage is hard, like
the light and noise of this birthplace.

The quiet sounds of night are our food;
our food is a trick, as if we didn't know.

In the night of night that the big ones
call dream, I see green, endless.

But that sweet retreat does not last;
each sunrise delivers me this world.

4

Two Nocturnal Tales

'The lamplight on the window made it look much darker outside than it really was.'

Tove Jansson, *The Summer Book*
(1972, trans Thomas Teal)

1

Under the Cover of Night: A Romance

They were standing outside the main building,
lunch over, a few students milling around.

'The third night is always the quietest,'
Ben said, the year-nine coordinator.

'Why do we do it to ourselves?' asked Rebecca.
'I don't mind school camp,' said Ben,

annoyingly chirpy. When he headed off
to the lake for kayaking, Rebecca felt

strangely empty and had a brief craving
for a cigarette. Two of her students,

Max and Paul from History, slouched past.
The boys had a cabin to themselves,

which Rebecca thought was a bad idea,
but there'd been some story in the staff room

that Max's father was 'gravely unwell'.
'Are you looking for somebody?' she called.

They stopped and turned. Paul shook his head.
'What group are you two in?' she asked.

They were both in Wandana. 'You'd better get
to the lake then. Mr Armstrong is already

down there,' she told them, not entirely convinced
about their intentions when they walked off.

**

After midnight, when everything was silent,
Max and Paul slipped out of their cabin.

The other cabins stood impassively in the night's light.
The trees made a rasping noise in the breeze.

Once Paul and Max got used to the darkness,
the night seemed to slip away.

The cold lighting and the pale moon
gave a ghostly illumination to the campsite.

Each footfall was amplified by the darkness.
'Walk on the asphalt,' whispered Max.

They walked down the smooth driveway,
through the vaguely Māori camp entrance,

and onto the unlit space of the main road.
'Christ, it's cold,' said Paul, shivering, despite himself.

Max pulled a small torch from his jeans
and traced an uncertain finger of light

across the apparition of the trees and
onto the oily blackness of the road.

They walked quickly and silently,
as if embarking on an arduous journey.

**

Rebecca was awake, vaguely unnerved
by the thought of all the sleeping bodies

in the silent cabins spread across the campsite.
She had another craving for a cigarette,

or some food. She imagined the calming glow
of an open fridge door at night, and thought of Ben.

It had taken her three years to get this job,
but after a moment she thought 'Fuck it',

and slipped out of bed. She made her way down
the cold corridor of the main building that

she and the other teachers shared, and gently
tapped on Ben's door. 'Are you mad?' he said,

letting her into the close dark of his room,
the white sheets of his bed a pale radioactive glow.

**

The service station was from another era.
It was completely unlit, but the phone booth

between the carpark and two old petrol pumps
shone in the darkness like a giant nightlight.

Paul moved away from the glare.
He turned to see Max entering the booth

and struggle to close the sliding door.
Max picked up the receiver, put a coin in the slot,

and dialed a number, apparently from memory.
From where Paul stood, under the ghost gums,

Max suddenly looked small, like somebody's
kid brother who had got into trouble.

Paul could see Max's lips move.
He was holding the phone like someone

in a tense scene in a movie,
or, Paul suddenly thought, like a child

talking to his parents, quietly begging
to be brought home. Then Max hung up

and quickly made his way back to Paul,
looking over his shoulder,

his feet crunching on the stones beside the road.
'Well?' said Paul. 'I got through,' said Max.

'They'll know it was you,' Paul replied.
'I made my voice sound different,' said Max.

'How did you do that?' asked Paul.
Max looked around at the dark trees

and the pale clouds above, as if really
seeing the night for the first time.

'What did you say, then?' asked Paul.
'I told them there was a bomb on site,' said Max.

'I told them they needed to get everyone out.
I told them it would go off in ten minutes.'

Paul and Max looked at each other for a moment,
then began to follow the road back to the camp.

When they got back, fifteen minutes later,
nothing had changed. The trees were silver;

they made discreet sounds in the night breeze.
The cold air smelt of eucalypt and dew.

Paul stared at Max, who ignored his look.
'I'm going back to bed,' Max said in his daytime voice.

**

Rebecca was in Ben's bed. 'Did you hear that?'
she said. 'I thought I heard something outside.'

Ben didn't reply, but the two of them stared,
first at the curtained window,

and then at the wooden door, as if
either of them could reveal something startling.

'You'd better get going,' Ben finally said,
in a neutral tone. He quietly sat up in bed,

as Rebecca picked about for her clothes.
'I wish I could stay here,'

she whispered when she was ready to go.
And then, leaning towards Ben's face in

the darkness, she said, 'Is this for real?'
'Is this the real thing, or just some hoax?'

2

La Notte: A Tale of the Uncanny

As for solitude, silence and darkness, all we can say is that these are factors connected with infantile anxiety, something that most of us never wholly overcome.

Sigmund Freud, 'The Uncanny' (1919)

I had recently experienced a period of ill health.
After the operation, my son stayed with me for a week
while I recuperated, and then I sent him back to his family.

(What indicators of identity do you want to know?
I will tell you only my age. I am sixty-two.
Not yet old, but no longer young. Not quite retired.)

It had been two years since the death of my spouse.
Some friends of mine had cared to hint that my illness
was an epiphenomenon of my bereavement.

(You might think that I am unduly cold,
my language overly technical, but I merely wish for
accuracy. I grieved badly when I was left alone.)

I had made it through the painful post-operative stage:
sleeping in the afternoon; walking the shuffling walk
of the injured; dreaming vividly. Not being myself.

(I read somewhere unlikely—a book on music,
perhaps—that it was common to experience a period
of cognitive disruption after a general anaesthetic.)

It was early spring and I was beginning to feel better.
One Saturday afternoon I decided to see a movie at the
local arthouse cinema: a re-run of Antonioni's *La Notte*.

(It is strange that one doesn't go to see films
alone more often; sitting in the dark, bathed in
light and sound, is ideally a solitary experience.)

At the end of the film, I felt strangely close to tears.
That final scene—the man kissing the woman in the bunker
of the golf course—was so grotesque, but somehow moving.

(The final panning away from the actors, across the trees
and the golf course, is typical Antonioni, who repeatedly
shows how people are ultimately to be put aside.)

When I returned home it was dusk and the phone was ringing.
It was my daughter. 'I've been to see *La Noche*,' I said.
She was confused for a moment. 'I mean *La Notte*.'

(My son and daughter each have a child just starting
to acquire language. Not enough has been written about
this miraculous process, this entry into being human.)

I didn't feel unduly upset about my little slip of the tongue,
but it took something of the shine away from the afternoon;
at my age anything can be taken for a sign.

(It is perhaps odd for siblings to procreate at the same time.
But given the age difference between my children, one can
only put it down to that universal condition, coincidence.)

I put off the performance of dinner, deciding
instead to have a lie down. Perhaps I had, after all,
overdone things a little by going out that afternoon.

(Time takes on a different quality when one lives alone;
the hours I sometimes longed for thirty years ago
can now feel like a ghostly presence in the house.)

I went into my bedroom, which used to be my son's,
about to lie down, when something caught my eye.
The small glass owl on the windowsill had been moved.

(I do not say 'had moved', since such objects can't move
by themselves. This goes without saying, I know, but I
want to make clear that this is not a supernatural story.)

I moved the piece of glass, small and smooth, back to
its proper place, a few centimetres towards the curtain.
I lay on the bed, pulled a blanket over myself, and fell asleep.

(As all children know, sleep is the annihilation of time.
Animals know this, too, filling their days with
the unfeeling state of unconsciousness.)

When I woke, it was night. As I stood before
the mirror in the darkened bathroom, washing
my hands, I felt the relief of not being in hospital.

(The windowless bathrooms in hospitals are
a form of entombment, or miniature versions
of those dread theatres at every hospital's centre.)

The next day, I called my son and, while on the phone,
noticed that something else, another small object,
had been inexplicably moved from its proper place.

(Talking on the phone is a vice of my generation.
My children, I know, would prefer I used text,
or even email, but I find both lacking in presence.)

This time the moved object was a small notebook
that I keep near the telephone. I write reminders in
the book, which was now on the dining table.

(My spouse used to love drawing in notepads, on bits
of paper, in the margins of newspapers—even
in the endpapers of books given to me as presents.)

I told my son about the two moving objects,
and he, unconcerned, said something about my memory,
as I knew inevitably he would.

(If ageing is a bad joke, as some say, then it is
because of the way it makes others treat us.
The ageing body both betrays and disguises.)

That week, I found five more objects that had been moved:
a book; an old pair of reading glasses; the key to the side gate;
a framed photograph of my parents; a knife.

(It is too easy, I am sure, to find symbolic weight
in this brief catalogue. The porous relationship between
the inner and outer worlds is an ancient theme.)

I briefly fantasised with the idea of seeing a private detective:
*no, I did not have a security system; yes, I sometimes
forget things; no, I don't have any known enemies.*

(Like most people, I suppose, I've never hired a detective.
Movies can't help but glamorise the shabby. I'm sure
that it would be not unlike visiting one's accountant.)

But I was less concerned with the unlikely possibility
of an intruder than with what might be happening
to my mind. Neurology, not criminology.

(Most people's faith in medical science is wildly
over-reaching. Such faith, I often think, is like
that of a child in a parent, who can make all better.)

I took myself to my doctor's untidy waiting room,
where I remembered the long party scene in *La Notte*,
the Italian bourgeoisie amusing themselves after dark.

(It was like an exaggerated version of the parties that my
extravagant parents used to hold. Do people still have parties
like that today? I suppose they must have them somewhere.)

I used to love those parties, how each thing in the house,
even the things in my bedroom, would be transformed
by the light and the guests, their noise and the music.

(I suddenly had a vision of my own house,
lit up in the suburban night, a party underway, the guests
all gently moving every object of my house a little to one side.)

This Voice

The hum of the late train
begins the night's soundtrack.
Bats make their ungodly
noise just outside your window,

above the distant growl of
trucks working down their gears.
A voice that could be yours
murmurs in your son's bedroom.

You bless everything
that is yours to lose,
a sunless bid for all the things
that go without saying.

Notes

'Documents' does not say enough about the staff of the Cardiac Ward at Geelong Hospital and Cardiology Services at Barwon Health, whose care was extraordinary, and to whom I am deeply indebted.

The story referred to in 'Animal Studies' is Lydia Davis's 'The Mouse'. It can be found in *The Collected Stories of Lydia Davis* (Penguin, 2014).

The book referred to in 'The Questionnaire' is Tomas Tranströmer's *Selected Poems: 1954-1986* (ed. Robert Hass, trans. Robert Bly et al, Ecco, 1987).

'Summer Nights, Walking' takes its title, among other things, from Robert Adams's photobook, *Summer Nights, Walking: Along the Colorado Front Range, 1976-1982* (Aperture Foundation/Yale University Art Gallery, 2009), which is an expanded edition of his *Summer Nights* (Aperture Foundation, 1985).

The epigraph to 'Election' is from Roberto Bolaño's *By Night in Chile* (trans. Chris Edwards, Vintage, 2009).

'"Whaling Station" Redux' refers to my poem 'Whaling Station' from *Outside* (Salt Publishing, 2011).

'Human Nature' (in 'Night Squibs') refers to *Last Words of the Executed* by Robert K Elder (University of Chicago Press, 2010).

'Apple Corps Ltd' was written without reference to *Good Ol' Freda* (2013), the documentary about Freda Kelly, 'secretary to the Beatles'. I do, though, recommend that charming film to anyone interested in the Beatles.

'Mick and Bianca Jagger, Newlyweds' is an ekphrastic poem based on a photograph by Patrick Lichfield.

'How to Be a Better Elvis' takes its title from a headline in *The Guardian*, 15th January 2014.

'Nightbird Singing' is one of a number of poems in 'Pastorals' that takes its title from a song. The various allusions to popular music throughout this section can be easily tracked using Google or any other web search engine.

'Before and After Science (Brian Eno in Hospital)' is based partly on Brian Eno's liner notes to his album *Discreet Music* (EG, 1975).

'Monody: Joni Mitchell Recalls Laurel Canyon' owes some small debts to John Milton's pastoral elegy, 'Lycidas' (1638).

As implied, 'Never For Ever' ends with a line from William Blake's *Visions of the Daughters of Albion* (1793).

'Bob Dylan's Ninth Eclogue' is a loose adaptation of lines from Virgil's Eclogue IX.

'Down Under' clearly owes a debt to the 1981 song of that name by Men at Work.

Acknowledgements

Poems in this collection have previously appeared in, or are soon to appear in, the *Hunter Anthology of Contemporary Australian Feminist Poetry* (ed. Bonny Cassidy & Jessica L. Wilkinson, in press), *The Western Australian Poetry Anthology* (ed. John Kinsella & Tracy Ryan, in press), *Writing to the Wire* (ed. Dan Disney & Kit Kelen, 2016), *The turnrow Anthology of Contemporary Australian Poetry* (ed. John Kinsella, 2014), *Australian Book Review*, *Australian Poetry Journal*, *Cordite Poetry Review*, *Double Dialogues*, *Snorkel*, *The Weekend Australian*, *Notes for the Translators: From 142 New Zealand and Australian Poets* (ed. Kit Kelen, 2012), the *Bittersweet Project* (Melbourne Writers' Festival, 2012), *The Best Australian Poems 2012* (ed. John Tranter), *The Best Australian Poems 2013* (ed. Lisa Gorton), *The Best Australian Poems 2014* (ed. Geoff Page), and *The Best Australian Poems 2015* (ed. Geoff Page). Audio versions of some of the poems in this collection were broadcast on ABC's Radio National and appear on my audio album *Outside Broadcast* (2013). My thanks to the relevant editors and broadcasters.

Thanks also to Yvonne Adami, Matthew Allen, Cassandra Atherton, Phillis Broadhurst, Kevin Brophy, Joel Deane, Tim Dolin, Lucy Dougan, Andrew Ford, Lisa Gorton, Kristin Headlam, Paul Hetherington, Paul Kane, John Kinsella, Amanda Johnson, Jo Langdon, Neil Levi, Cameron Lowe, Anthony Lynch, John McCooey, Phillis McCooey, Michael Myshack, Felicity Plunkett, Peter Rose, Tracy Ryan, Craig Sherborne, Chris Wallace-Crabbe, and Chris Wortham (who did not teach me Middle English), and to Kate McCooey and Sam Takolander. Thank you to Terri-ann White for pushing me.

I am privileged to have Maria Takolander as my first reader and collaborator.